The His

Remarkable Life of John

Sheppard

Containing a Particular Account of His Many Robberies and EscapesBook Name

Daniel Defoe

Alpha Editions

ISBN : 9789353291235

Design and Setting By
Alpha Editions
email - alphaedis@gmail.com

THE HISTORY

Of the remarkable LIFE of

JOHN SHEPPARD,

CONTAINING

A particular Account of his many ROBBERIES and ESCAPES,

Viz,.

His robbing the Shop of Mr. *Bains* in White-Horse-Yard of 24 Yards of Fustian. Of his breaking and entering the House of the said Mr. *Bains*, and stealing in Goods and Money to the Value of 20 l. Of his robbing the House of Mr. *Charles* in *May Fair* of Money, Rings, Plate, &c to the Value of 30 l. Of his robbing the House of Mrs. *Cook* in *Clare-Market,* along with his pretended Wife, and his Brother, to the Value of between 50 and 60 l. Of his breaking the Shop of Mr. *Philips* in *Drury-Lane,* with the same Persons, and stealing Goods of small Value. Of his entering the House of Mr. *Carter,* a Mathematical Instrument Maker in *Wytch Street,* along with *Anthony Lamb* and *Charles Grace,* and robbing of Mr. *Barton,* a Master Taylor who lodged therein, of Goods and Bonds to the Value of near 300 l. Of his breaking and entering the House of Mr. *Kneebone,* a Woollen-Draper, near the *New Church* in the *Strand,* in Company of *Joseph Blake* alias *Blewskin* and *William Field,* and stealing Goods to the Value of near 50 l. Of his robbing of Mr. *Pargiter* on the Highway near the Turnpike, on the Road *Hampstead,* along with the said *Blewskin.* Of his robbing a Lady's Woman in her Mistress's Coach on the same Road. Of his robbing also a Stage Coach, with the said *Blewskin,* on the *Hampstead* Road. Likewise of his breaking the Shop of Mr. *Martin* in *Fleet-street,* and stealing 3 silver Watches of 15 l. Value.

ALSO—

A particular Account of his rescuing his pretended Wife from St. *Giles's* Round House. Of the wonderful Escape himself made from the said Round-House. Of the miraculous Escape he and his said pretended Wife made together from *New-Prison,* on the 25th of *May* last. Of his surprizing Escape from the Condemn'd Hold of *Newgate* on the 31st of *August.* Together with the true manner of his being retaken; and of his Behaviour in *Newgate,* till the most astonishing, and never to be forgotten Escape he made from thence, in the Night of the 15th of October. The Whole taken from the most authentick

Accounts, as the Informations of divers Justices of the Peace, the several Shop-keepers above-mentioned, the principal Officers of *Newgate* and *New Prison*, and from the Confession of *Sheppard* made to the Rev. Mr. *Wagstaff*, who officiated for the Ordinary at *Newgate*.

TO THE CITIZENS
OF
London and Westminster

GENTLEMEN,

Experience has confirm'd you in that everlasting Maxim, *that there is no other way to protect the* Innocent, *but by Punishing the* Guilty.

Crimes ever were, and ever must be unavoidably frequent in such populous Cities as yours are, being the necessary Consequences, either of the Wants, *or the Depravity, of the lowest part of the* humane *Species.*

At this time the most flagrant Offences, as Burning of Dwellings; Burglaries, *and* Highway Robberies *abound; and* Frauds *common* Felonies, *and* Forgeries *are practic'd without Number; thus not only your Properties, but even your very Lives are every way struck at.*

The Legislative Power *has not been wanting in providing necessary and wholesome Laws against these* Evils, *the executive part whereof (according to your great Privileges) is lodged in your own Hands: And the Administration hath at all times applyed proper Remedies and Regulations to the* Defects *which have happen'd in the* Magistracy *more immediately under their Jurisdiction.*

Through the just and salutary Severities of the Magistrates, publick excessive Gaming *has been in a manner Surpress'd; and some late Examples of divine Vengeance have overtaken certain of the most notorious lewd* Prostitutes *of the Town, which together with the laudable endeavours of the great and worthy* Societies, *has given no small check to that enormous and spreading* Vice.

But here's a Criminal *bids Defiance to your* Laws, *and* Justice *who declar'd and has manifested that the* Bars *are not made that can either keep him* Out, *or keep him* In, *and accordingly hath a second time fled from the very* Bosom Of Death.

His History will astonish! and is not compos'd of Fiction, Fable, or Stories plac'd at York, Rome, *or* Jamaica, *but* Facts *done at your Doors,* Facts *unheard of, altogether new, Incredible, and yet Uncontestable.*

He is gone once more upon his wicked Range in the World. Restless Vengeance is pursuing, and Gentlemen *'tis to be hoped that she will be assisted by your Endeavours to bring to Justice this notorious Offender.*

THE LIFE OF
JOHN SHEPPARD, &c.

This *John Sheppard*, a Youth both in Age and Person, tho' an old Man in Sin; was Born in the Parish of *Stepney* near *London*, in the Year 1702, a Son, Grandson, and great Grandson of a *Carpenter*. His Father died when he was so very Young that he could not recollect that ever he saw him. Thus the burthen of his Maintenance, together with his Brother's and Sister's, lay upon the Shoulders of the Widow Mother, who soon procured an Admittance of her Son *John* into the *Work-House* in *Bishopsgate-street*, where he continued for the space of a Year and half, and in that time received an Education sufficient to qualifie him for the Trade his Mother design'd him, *viz.* a *Carpenter*. Accordingly she was recommended to Mr. *Wood* in *Witch-Street* near *Drury-Lane*, as a Master capable of entertaining and instructing her Son: They agreed and Bound he was for the space of seven Years; the Lad proved an early proficient, had a ready and ingenious Hand, and soon became Master of his Business, and gave entire Satisfaction to his Master Customers, and had the Character of a very sober and orderly Boy. But alas unhappy Youth! before he had compleated six Years of his Apprenticeship, he commenced a fatal Acquaintance with one *Elizabeth Lyon*, otherwise call'd *Edgworth Bess*, from a Town of that Name in *Middlesex* where she was Born, the reputed Wife of a Foot Soldier, and who lived a wicked and debauch'd Life; and our young *Carpenter* became Enamour'd of her, and they must Cohabit together as Man and Wife.

Now was laid the Foundation of his Ruin; *Sheppard* grows weary of the Yoke of Servitude, and began to dispute with his Master; telling him that his way of Jobbing from House to House was not sufficient to furnish him with a due Experience in his Trade; and that if he would not set out to undertake some Buildings, he would step into the World for better Information. Mr. *Wood* a mild, sober, honest Man, indulg'd him; and Mrs. *Wood* with Tears, exhorted him against the Company of this lewd Prostitute: But her Man prompted and harden'd by his HARLOT, D—— n'd *her Blood*, and threw a Stick at his Mistress, and beat her to the Ground. And being with his Master at Work at Mr. *Britt's* the *Sun* Ale-house near *Islington*, upon a very trivial Occasion fell upon his Master, and beat and bruised him in a most barbarous and shameful Manner. Such a sudden and deplorable Change was there in the Behaviour of this promising young Man. Next ensued a neglect of Duty, both to God and his Master, lying out of Nights, perpetual Jarrings, and Animosities; these and such like, were the Consequences of his intimacy with this she *Lyon*; who by the sequel will appear to have been a main loadstone in attracting of him up to this Eminence of Guilt.

Mr. *Wood* having Reason to suspect, that *Sheppard* had robb'd a Neighbour, began to be in great Fear and Terror for himself. And when his Man came not Home in due season at Nights bar'd him out; but he made a mere jest of the Locks and Bolts, and enter'd in, and out at Pleasure; and when Mr. *Wood* and his Wife have had all the Reason in the World to believe him Lock't out, they have found him very quiet in his Bed the next Morning, such was the power of his early Magick.

Edgworth Bess having stol'n a Gold Ring from a Gentleman, whom she had pick'd up in the Streets, was sent to St. *Giles's* Round-house; *Sheppard* went immediately to his Consort, and after a short Discourse with Mr. *Brown* the Beadle, and his Wife, who had the Care of the Place, he fell upon the poor old Couple, took the Keys from them, and let his Lady out at the Door in spight of all the Out-cryes, and Opposition they were capable of making.

About *July* 1723, He was by his Master sent to perform a Repair, at the House of Mr. *Bains*, a Piece-Broker in *White-Horse Yard*; he from thence stole a Roll of Fustain, containing 24 Yards, which was afterwards found in his Trunk. This is supposed to be the first Robbery he ever committed and it was not long e're he Repeated another upon this same Mr. *Bains*, by breaking into his House in the Night-time, and taking out of the *Till* seven Pounds in Money, and Goods to the value of fourteen Pounds more. How he enter'd this House, was a Secret till his being last committed to *Newgate*, when he confessed that he took up the Iron Bars at the Cellar Window, and after he had done his Business, he nailed them down again, so that Mr. *Bains* never believed his House had been broke;

and an innocent Woman a Lodger in the House lay all the while under the weight of a suspicion of committing the Robbery.

Sheppard and his Master had now parted, ten Months before the expiration of his Apprenticeship, a woeful parting to the former; he was gone from a good and careful Patronage, and lay expos'd to, and comply'd with the Temptations of the most wicked Wretches this Town could afford as *Joseph Blake*, alias *Blewskins*, *William Field, Doleing, James Sykes*, alias *Hell* and *Fury*, which last was the first that betray'd, and put him into the Hands of Justice, as will presently appear.

Having deserted his Master's Service, he took Shelter in the House of Mr. *Charles* in *May-Fair*, near *Piccadilly*, and his Landlord having a Necessity for some Repairs in his House, engag'd one Mr. *Panton* a *Carpenter* to Undertake them, and *Sheppard* to assist him as a Journeyman; but on the 23rd of *October*, 1723, e're the Work was compleat, *Sheppard* took Occasion to rob the People of the Effects following, *viz*. seven Pound ten Shillings in Specie, five large silver Spoons, six plain Forks ditto, four Tea-Spoons, six plain Gold Rings, and a Cypher Ring; four Suits of Wearing Apparel, besides Linnen, to a considerable value. This Fact he confess'd to the Reverend Mr. *Wagstaff* before his Escape from the Condemn'd Hold of *Newgate*.

Sheppard had a Brother, nam'd *Thomas*, a *Carpenter* by Profession, tho' a notorious Thief and House-breaker by Practice. This *Thomas* being committed to *Newgate* for breaking the House of Mrs. *Mary Cook* a *Linnen-Draper*, in *Clare-street, Clare-Market*, on the 5th of *February* last, and stealing Goods to the value of between 50, and 60 l. he impeach'd his Brother *John Sheppard*, and *Edgworth Bess* as being concerned with him in the Fact; and these three were also Charg'd with being concern'd together, in breaking the House of Mr. *William Phillips* in *Drury-Lane*, and stealing divers Goods, the Property of Mrs. *Kendrick* a Lodger in the House, on the 14th of the said *February*: All possible endeavours were us'd by Mrs. *Cook* and Mr. *Phillips*, to get *John Sheppard* and *Edgworth Bess* Apprehended, but to no purpose, till the following Accident.

Sheppard was now upon his wicked Range in *London*, committing Robberies every where at Discretion; but one Day meeting with his Acquaintance, *James Sykes*, alias *Hell* and *Fury*, sometimes a Chairman, and at others a Running Foot-man. This *Sykes* invited him to go to one *Redgate's*, a Victualling-house near the *Seven Dials*, to play at *Skettles*, *Sheppard* comply'd, and *Sykes* secretly sent for Mr. *Price* a Constable in St. *Giles's Parish*, and Charg'd him with his Friend *Sheppard* for the Robbing of Mrs. *Cook*, &c. *Sheppard* was carried before Justice *Parry*, who order'd him to St. *Giles's* Round-house till the next Morning for farther Examination: He was Confin'd in the Upper part of the Place, being two Stories from the Ground, but 'ere two Hours came about, by only the help of a Razor, and the Stretcher of a Chair, he broke open the Top of the Round house, and tying together a Sheet and Blanket, by them descended into the Church-yard and Escap'd, leaving the Parish to Repair the Damage, and Repent of the Affront put upon his Skill and Capacity.

On the 19th of *May* last in the Evening, *Sheppard* with another Robber named *Benson*, were passing thro' *Leicester-fields*, where a Gentleman stood accusing a Woman with an attempt to steal his Watch, a Mobb was gathered about the Disputants, and *Sheppard's* Companion being a *Master*, got in amongst them and pick'd the Gentleman's Pocket in good earnest of the Watch; the Scene was surprizingly chang'd, from an imaginary Robbery to a real one; and in a moment ensued an Out-cry of *stop Thief*, *Sheppard* and *Benson* took to their Heels, and *Sheppard* was seiz'd by a Serjeant of the Guard at *Leicester* House, crying out *stop Thief* with much earnestness. He was convey'd to St. *Ann's Round House* in *Soho*, and kept secure till the next Morning, when *Edgworth Bess* came to visit him, who was seiz'd also; they were carried before Justice *Walters*, when the People in *Drury-Lane* and *Clare-Market* appeared, and charged them with the Robberies aforemention'd: But *Sheppard* pretending to Impeach certain of his Accomplices, the Justice committed them to *New-Prison*, with intent to have them soon removed to *Newgate*, unless there came from them some useful Discoveries. *Sheppard* was now a second time in the hands of Justice, but how long he intended to keep in them, the Reader will soon be able to Judge.

He and his MATE were now in a strong and well guarded Prison, himself loaded with a pair of double *Links* and *Basils*[17] of about fourteen pounds weight, and confined together in the safest Appartment call'd *Newgate Ward*; *Sheppard* conscious of his Crimes, and knowing the *Information* he had made to be but a blind

Amusement that would avail him nothing; he began to Meditate an Escape. They had been thus detained for about four Days, and their Friends having the Liberty of seeing them, furnish'd him with Implements proper for his Design, accordingly Mr. *Sheppard* goes to work, and on the 25th of May being *Whit-son Monday* at about two of the Clock in the Morning, he had compleated a practicable breach, and sawed of his Fetters; having with unheard of Diligence and Dexterity, cut off an Iron Bar from the Window, and taken out a Muntin, or Bar of the most solid Oak of about nine Inches in thickness, by boring it thro' in many Places, a work of great Skill and Labour; they had still five and twenty Foot to descend from the Ground; *Sheppard* fasten'd a Sheet and Blanket to the Bars, and causes Madam to take off her Gown and Petticoat, and sent her out first, and she being more Corpulent than himself, it was with great Pain and Difficulty that he got her through the Interval, and observing his Directions, was instantly down, and more frighted than hurt; the *Phylosopher* follow'd, and lighted with Ease and Pleasure; But where are they Escap'd to? Why out of one Prison into another. The Reader is to understand, that the *New Prison* and *Clerkenwell Bridewell* lye Contiguous to one another, and they are got into the Yard of the latter, and have a Wall of twenty-two Foot high to Scale, before their Liberty is perfected; *Sheppard* far from being unprepared to surmount this Difficulty, has his Gimblets and Peircers ready, and makes a Scaleing-Ladder. The Keepers and Prisoners of both Places are a sleep in their Beds; he Mounts his *Bagage*, and in less than ten Minutes carries both her and himself over this wall, and compleats an entire Escape. Altho' his Escape from the Condemn'd Hold of *Newgate*, has made a far greater Noise in the World, than that from this Prison hath. It has been allow'd by all the Jayl-Keepers in *London*, that one so Miraculous was never perform'd before in *England*; the broken Chains and Bars are kept at *New Prison* to Testifie, and preserve the Memory of this extraordinary Villain.

Sheppard not warn'd by this Admonition, returns like a *Dog to his Vomit*, and comes Secretly into his Master *Wood's* Neighbourhood in *Witch-street*, and conceits Measures with one *Anthony Lamb*, an Apprentice to Mr. *Carter* a Mathematical Instrument-maker, for Robbing of Mr. *Barton* a Master Taylor; a Man of Worth and Reputation, who Lodg'd in Mr. *Carter's* House. *Charles Grace*, a graceless Cooper was let into the Secret, and consented, and resolved to Act his Part. The 16th of *June* last was appointed, *Lamb* accordingly lets *Grace* and *Sheppard* into the House at Mid-Night; and they all go up to Mr. *Bartons* Appartment well arm'd with Pistols, and enter'd his Rooms, without being disturb'd. *Grace* was Posted at Mr. *Barton's* Bedside with a loaded Pistol, and positive Orders to shoot him through the Head, if in case he awak'd. *Sheppard* being engag'd in opening the Trunks and Boxes, the mean while. It luckily happen'd for Mr. *Barton*, that he slept Sounder than usual that Night, as having come from a Merry-making with some Friends; tho' poor Man little Dreaming in what dreadful Circumstances. They carried off in Notes, and Bonds, Guineas, Cloaths, Made and Unmade, to the value of between two and three Hundred Pounds; besides a Padesuoy Suit of Cloaths, worth about eighteen or twenty Pounds more; which having been made for a Corpulent Gentleman, *Sheppard* had them reduc'd, and fitted for his own Size and War, as designing to Appear and make a Figure among the *Beau Monde*. *Grace* and *Sheppard*, having disposed of the Goods at an Ale-house in *Lewkenors Lane* (a Rendezvous of Robbers and Ruffians) took their Flight, and *Grace* had not been since heard of. *Lamb* was apprehended, and carried before Justice *Newton*, and made an ample Confession; and there being nothing but that against him at his Tryal, and withal, a favourable Prosecution, he came off with a Sentence of Transportation only. He as well as *Sheppard* has since confirm'd all the above particulars, and with this Addition, *viz.* That it was Debated among them to have Murder'd all the People in the House, save one Person.

About the latter End of the same Month, *June*, Mr. *Kneebone*, a Woollen-Draper near the New Church in the *Strand*, receiv'd a Caution from the Father of *Anthony Lamb*, who intimated to Mr. *Kneebone* that his House was intended to be broke open and robb'd that very Night. Mr. *Kneebone* prepar'd for the Event, ordering his Servants to sit up, and gave Directions to the Watchman in the Street to observe his House: At about two in the Morning *Sheppard* and his Gang were about the Door, a Maid-Servant went to listen, and heard one of the Wretches, say, *Da—n him, if they could not enter that Night, they would another, and would have 300l. of his*, (meaning) Mr. *Kneebone's* Money. They went off, and nothing more was heard of them till *Sunday* the 12th Day of *July* following, when *Joseph Blake*, alias *Blewskins, John Sheppard*, and *William Field* (as himself Swears) came about 12 o'clock at Night, and cut two large Oaken-Bars over the Cellar-Window, at the back part of the House in *Little-Drury-Lane*, and so entered; Mr. *Kneebone*, and his Family being at Rest, they proceeded to open a Door at the Foot of the Cellar-Stairs, with three Bolts, and a large Padlock upon it, and then came up into the Shop and wrench'd off the Hasp, and Padlock that went over the Press, and arriv'd at their desir'd Booty; they continu'd in the House for three Hours, and carry'd off with them One Hundred and eight Yards of Broad Woollen Cloth, five Yards of blue Bays, a light Tye-Wig, and Beaver-Hat, two Silver Spoons, an Handkerchief, and a Penknife. In all to the value of near fifty Pounds.

The *Sunday* following, being the 19th of *July, Sheppard* and *Blewskins* were out upon the *Hampstead* Road, and there stopt a Coach with a Ladies Woman in it, from whom they took but Half-a-Crown; all the Money then about her; the Foot-man behind the Coach came down, and exerted himself; but *Sheppard* sent him in hast up to his Post again, by threat of his Pistol.

The next Night being the 20th of *july*, about Nine, they Robb'd Mr. *Pargiter*, a Chandler of *Hamstead*, near the Halfway-House; *Sheppard* after his being taken at *Finchley* was particularly examin'd about this Robbery. The Reverend Mr. *Wagstaff* having receiv'd a Letter from an unknown Hand, with two Questions, to be propos'd to *Sheppard, viz.* Whether he did Rob *John Pargiter*, on *Monday* the 20th of *July*, about Nine at Night, between the *Turnpike* and *Hamstead*; How much Money he took from him? Whither *Pargiter* was Drunk, or not, and if he had Rings or Watch about him, when robb'd? which, Request was comply'd with, and *Sheppard* affirm'd, that Mr. *Pargiter* was very much in Liquor, having a great Coat on; neither Rings on his Fingers or Watch, and only three Shillings in his Pocket, which they took from him, and that *Blewskins* knock him down twice with the Butt-end of his Pistol to make sure Work, (tho' Excess of drink had done that before) but *Sheppard* did in kindness raise him up as often.

The next Night, *July* 21, they stopt a Stage-Coach, and took from a Passenger in it, Twenty-two Shillings, and were so expeditious in the Matter, that *not two Words were made about the Bargain.*

Now Mr. *Sheppard's* long and wicked Course seemingly draws towards a Period. Mr. *Kneebone* having apply'd to *Jonathan Wild*, and set forth Advertisements in the Papers, complaining of his Robbery. On *Tuesday* the 22d of *July* at Night *Edgworth Bess* was taken in a Brandy-shop, near *Temple-Bar* by *Jonathan Wild*; she being much terrify'd, discover'd where *Sheppard* was: A Warrant was accordingly issued by Justice *Blackerby*, and the next Day he was Apprehended, at the House of *Blewskin's* Mother, in *Rose-Mary-Lane*, by one *Quilt*, a Domestick of Mr. *Wild's* though not without great opposition, for, he clapt a loaded, Pistol to *Quilt's* Breast, and attempted to shoot him, but the Pistol miss'd fire; he was brought back to *New Prison*, confin'd in the Dungeon; and the next Day carried before Justice *Blackerby*. Upon his Examination he Confess'd the three Robberies on the Highway aforemention'd, as also the Robbing of Mr. *Bains*, Mr. *Barton*, and Mr. *Kneebone*, he was committed to Newgate, and at the Sessions of *Oyer* and *Terminer*, and Goal delivery, holden at the *Old-Baily*, on the 12th, 13th and 14th of *August*, he was try'd upon three several indictments, *viz*. First for breaking the House of *William Philips*.

John Sheppard, of the Parish of St. *Martin* in *the Fields*, was indicted for breaking the House of *William Philips*, and stealing divers Goods, the 14th of *February* last. But there not being sufficient Evidence against the Prisoner, he was acquitted.

He was also indicted a Second Time, of St. *Clement Danes*, for breaking the House of *Mary Cook*, the 5th of *February* last, and stealing divers Goods: But the Evidence against the Prisoner being defficient as to this Indictment also, he was acquitted.

He was also indicted the Third Time, of St. *Mary Savoy*, for breaking the House of *William Kneebone*, in the Night-Time, and stealing, 108 Yards of Woollen Cloth, the 12th of *July* last. The Prosecutor depos'd, That the Prisoner had some Time since been his Servant, and when he went to Bed, the Time mentioned in the Indictment, about 11 a-Clock at Night, he saw all the Doors and Windows fast; but was call'd up about four in the Morning, and found his House broke open, the Bars of a Cellar-Window having been cut, and the Bolts of the Door that comes up Stairs drawn, and the Padlock wrench'd off, and the Shutter in the Shop broken, and his Goods gone; whereupon suspecting the Prisoner, he having committed ill Actions thereabouts before, he acquainted *Jonathan Wild* with it, and he procur'd him to be apprehended. That he went to the Prisoners in New *Prison*, and asking how he could be so ungrateful to rob him, after he had shown him so much Kindness? The Prisoner own'd he had been ungrateful in doing so, informing him of several Circumstances as to the Manner of committing the Fact, but said he had been drawn into it by ill Company. *Jonathan Wild*, depos'd, The Prosecutor came to him, and desir'd him to enquire after his Goods that had been stolen, telling him he suspected the Prisoner to have been concern'd in the Robbery, he having before committed some Robberies in the Neighbourhood. That inquiring after him, and having heard of him before, he was inform'd that he was an Acquaintance of *Joseph Blake*, alias *Blewskins*, and *William Field*: Whereupon he sent for *William Field*, who came to him; upon which he told him, if he would make an ingenuous Confession, he believ'd he could prevail with the Court to make him an Evidence. That he did make a Discovery of the Prisoner, upon which he was apprehended, and also of others since convicted, and gave an Account of some Parcels of the Cloth, which were found accordingly. *William Field* depos'd, That the Prisoner told him, and *Joseph Blake*, that he knew a *Ken* where they might get something of Worth. That they went to take a View of the Prosecutor's House, but disprov'd of the Attempt, as not thinking it easy to be perform'd; But the Prisoner perswaded them that it might easily be done, he knowing the House, he having liv'd with the Prosecutor. That thereupon he cut the Cellar Bar, went into the Cellar, got into the Shop, and brought out three Parcels of Cloth, which they carried away. The Prisoner had also confest the Fact when he was apprehended, and before the Justice. The Fact being plainly prov'd, the Jury found him guilty of the Indictment.

Sentence of Death was pronounc'd upon him accordingly. Several other Prosecutions might have been brought against him, but this was thought sufficient to rid the World of so Capital an Offender: He beg'd earnestly for Transportation, to the most extream Foot of his Majesty's Dominions; and pleaded Youth, and Ignorance as the Motive which had precipitated him into the Guilt; but the Court deaf to his Importunities, as knowing him, and his repeated Crimes to be equally flagrant, gave him no satisfactory Answer: He return'd to his dismal Abode the Condemn'd Hold, where were Nine more unhappy Wretches in as dreadful Circumstances as himself. The Court being at *Windsor*, the Malefactors had a longer Respite than is usual; during that Recess, *James Harman*, *Lumley*,

Davis and *Sheppard* agreed upon an Escape, concerted Measures, and provided Instruments to make it effectual; but put off the Execution of their Design, on Account the two Gentlemen having their hopes of Life daily renewed by the favourable Answers they receiv'd from some considerable Persons; but those vanishing the day before their Execution, and finding their Sentence irreversible, they two dropt their hopes, together with the Design, they form'd for an Escape, and so in earnest prepar'd to meet Death on the Morrow, (which they accordingly did.). 'Twas on this Day Mr *Davis* gave *Sheppard* the Watch Springs, Files, Saws, *&c.* to Effect his own Release; and knowing that a Warrant was Hourly expected for his Execution with Two others, on the *Friday* following; he thought it high time to look about him, for he had waited his Tryal, saw his Conviction, and heard his Sentence with some patience; but finding himself irrespitably decreed for Death, he could sit passive no longer, and on the very Day of the Execution of the former; whilst they were having their Fetters taken off, in order for going to the Tree, that Day he began to saw, *Saturday* made a progress; but *Sunday* omitted, by Reason of the Concourse in the *Lodge*: *Edgworth Bess* having been set at Liberty, had frequent Access to him, with others of his Acquaintance. On *Monday* the Death *Warrant* came from *Windsor*, appointing that he, together with *Joseph Ward* and *Anthony Upton* should be Executed on the *Friday* following, being the 4th of *September*. The Keepers acquainted him therewith, and desired him to make good use of that short Time. He thank'd them, said *he would follow their Advice*, and *prepare*. *Edgworth Bess*, and another Woman had been with him at the Door of the Condemn'd Hold best part of the Afternoon, between five and six he desir'd the other Prisoners, except *Stephen Fowles* to remain above, while he offer'd something in private to his Friends at the Door; they comply'd, and in this interval he got the Spike asunder, which made way for the Skeleton to pass with his Heels foremost, by the Assistance of *Fowles*, whom he most ungenerously betray'd to the Keepers after his being retaken, and the Fellow was as severely punish'd for it.

Having now got clear of his Prison, he took Coach disguis'd in a Night Gown at the corner of the *Old Baily*, along with a Man who waited for him in the Street (and is suppos'd to be *Page* the Butcher) ordering the Coachman to drive to *Black-Fryers Stairs*, where his prostitute gave him the Meeting, and they three took

Boat, and went a Shoar at the *Horse-Ferry* at *Westminster*, and at the *White-Hart* they went in, Drank, and stay'd sometime; thence they adjourn'd to a Place in *Holbourn*, where by the help of a Saw he quitted the Chains he had brought with him from *Newgate*; and then like a Freeman took his Ramble through the City and came to *Spittle-Fields*, and there lay with *Edgeworth Bess*.

It may be easy to imagine what an alarm his Escape gave to the Keepers of *Newgate*, three of their People being at the farther End of the *Lodge*, engag'd in a Discourse concerning his wonderful Escape from *New-Prison*, and what Caution ought to be us'd, lest he should give them the slip, at that very Instant as he perfected it.

On *Tuesday* he sent for *William Page* an Apprentice to a Butcher in *Clare-Market*, who came to him, and being Pennyless, he desir'd *Page* to give him what Assistance he could to make his way, and being a Neighbour and Acquaintance, he comply'd with it; but e're he would do any thing, he consulted a near Relation, who as he said, encourag'd him in it; nay, put him upon it, so meeting with this Success in his Application to his Friend, and probable an Assistance in the Pocket, he came to *Sheppard* having bought him a new blue *Butcher's* Frock, and another for himself, and so both took their Rout to *Warnden* in *Northamptonshire*, where they came to a Relation of *Page's*, who receiv'd and Entertain'd them kindly, the People lying from their own Bed to Accommodate them. *Sheppard* pretending to be a *Butcher's* Son in *Clare-Market*, who was going farther in the Country to his Friends, and that *Page* was so kind as to Accompany him; but they as well as their Friend became tir'd of one another; the *Butchers* having but one Shilling left, and the People poor, and Consequently unable to Subsist two such Fellows, after a stay of three or four Days, they return'd, and came for *London*, and reach'd the City on *Tuesday* the 8th of *September*, calling by the way at *Black-Mary's-Hole*, and Drinking with several of their Acquaintance, and then came into *Bishopsgate street*, to one *Cooley's* a *Brandy-shop*; where a *Cobler* being at Work in his Stall, stept out and Swore *ther was* Sheppard, *Sheppard* hearing him, departed immediately. In the Evening they came into *Fleet-street*, at about Eight of the Clock, and observing Mr. *Martins* a Watchmaker's Shop to be open, and a little Boy only to look after it: *Page* goes in and asks the Lad whether Mr. *Taylor* a *Watchmaker* lodg'd in the House? being answer'd in the Negative, he came away, and Reports the Disposition of the Place: *Sheppard* now makes Tryal of his old Master-peice; fixeth a Nail Peircer into the Door post, fastens the Knocker thereto with Packthread, breaks the Glass, and takes out three *Silver Watches* of 15 l. value, the Boy seeing him take them, but could not get out to pursue him, by reason of his Contrivance. One of the Watches he Pledg'd for a Guinea and Half. The same Night they came into *Watch-street, Sheppard* going into his *Master's* Yard, and calling for his Fellow 'Prentice, his Mistress heard, knew his Voice, and was dreadfully frightened; he next went to the *Cock* and *Pye Ale-House* in *Drury-Lane*, sent for a Barber his Acquaintance, drank Brandy and eat Oysters in the view of several people. *Page* waiting all the while at the Door, the whole Neighbourhood being alarm'd, yet none durst attempt him, for fear of Pistols, *&c.* He had vow'd Revenge upon a poor Man as kept a Dairy-Cellar, at the End of *White-Horse-Yard*, who having seen him at *Islington* after his Escape, and engag'd not to speak of it, broke his Promise; wherefore *Sheppard* went to his Residence took the Door off the Hinges and threw it down amongst all the Man's Pans, Pipkins, and caus'd a Deluge of Cream and Milk all over the Cellar.

This Night he had a narrow Escape, one Mr. *Ireton* a Sheriffs Officer seeing him and *Page* pass thro' *Drury-Lane*, at about Ten o'clock pursu'd 'em, and laid hold of *Page* instead of *Sheppard*, who got off, thus *Ireton*, missing the main Man, and thinking *Page* of no Consequence, let him go after him.

Edgworth Bess had been apprehended by *Jonathan Wild*, and by Sir *Francis Forbes* one of the Aldermen of *London*, committed to the *Poultry-Compter*, for being aiding and assisting to *Sheppard* in his Escape; the Keepers and others terrify'd and purg'd her as much as was possible to discover where he was, but had it been in her Inclination, it was not in her Power so to do, as it manifestly appear'd soon after.

The People about the *Strand, Witch-street* and *Drury-Lane*, whom he had Robb'd, and who had prosecuted him were under great Apprensions and Terror, and in particular Mr. *Kneebone*, on whom he vow'd a bloody Revenge; because he refus'd to sign a Petition in his behalf to the *Recorder* of *London*. This Gentleman was forc'd to keep arm'd People up in his House every Night till he was Re-taken, and had the same fortify'd in the strongest manner. Several other Shop-keepers in this Neighbourhood were also put to great Expence and Trouble to Guard themselves against this dreadful Villian.

The Keepers of *Newgate*, whom the rash World loaded with Infamy, stigmatiz'd and branded with the Title of Persons guilty of Bribery; for Connivance at his Escape, they and what Posse in their Power, either for Love or Money did Contribute their utmost to undeceive a wrong notion'd People. Their Vigilance was remarkably indefatigable, sparing neither Money nor Time, Night nor Day to bring him back to his deserv'd Justice. After many Intelligences, which they endeavour'd for, and receiv'd, they had one which prov'd very Successful. Having learnt for a certainty that their Haunts was about *Finchly Common*, and being very well assur'd of the very House where they lay; on *Thursday* the 10th of *September*, a posse of Men, both of Spirit and Conduct, furnish'd with Arms proper for their Design, went for *Finchley*, some in a Coach and Four, and others on Horseback. They dispers'd themselves upon the *Common* aforesaid, in order to make their View, where they had not been long e're they came in Sight of *SHEPPARD* in Company of *WILLIAM PAGE*, habited like two *Butchers* in new blue Frocks, with white Aprons tuck'd round their Wastes.

Upon *Sheppard's* seeing *Langley* a Turnkey at *Newgate*, he says to his Companion *Page, I see a Stag*; upon which their Courage dropt; knowing that now their dealing way of Business was almost at an End; however to make their Flight as secure as they could, they thought it adviseable to take to a Foot-path, to cut off the pursuit of the *Newgate Cavalry*; but this did not prove most successful, *Langley* came up with *Page* (who was hindermost) and Dismounting with Pistol in Hand, commands *Page* to throw up his Hands, which he trembling did, begging for Life, desiring him to *Fisk* him, *viz*. (search him,) which he accordingly did, and found a broad Knife and File; having thus disarm'd him, he takes the *Chubb* along with him in quest of the slippery *Ele, Sheppard*; who had taken Shelter in an old Stable, belonging to a Farm-House; the pursuit was close, the House invested, and a Girl seeing his Feet as he stood up hid, discover'd him. *Austin* a Turnkey first attach'd his Person. *Langley* seconded him, *Ireton* an Officer help'd to Enclose, and happy was the hindermost who aided in this great Enterprise. He being shock'd with the utmost Fear, told them he submitted, and desir'd they would let him live as long as he could, which they did, and us'd him mildly; upon searching him they found a broad Knife with two of the Watches as he had taken out of Mr. *Martin's* Shop, one under each Armpit; and now having gain'd their Point, and made themselves Masters of what they had often endeavoured for, they came with their *Lost Sheep* to a little House on the *Common* that sold Liquors, with this Inscription on the Sign, *I have brought my Hogs to a fair Market*; which our two unfortunate *Butchers* under their then unhappy Circumstances, had too sad Reason to apply to themselves. *Sheppard* had by this time recover'd his Surprize, grew calm and easy, and desir'd them to give him Brandy, they did, and were all good Friends, and Company together.

They adjourn'd with their Booty to another Place, where was waiting a Coach and Four to Convey it to Town, with more Speed and Safety; and Mr. *Sheppard* arriv'd at his old Mansion, at about two in the Afternoon. At his a-lighting, he made a sudden Spring; He declar'd his Intention was to have slipt under the Coach, and had a Race for it; he was put into the Condemn'd-Hold, and Chain'd down to the Floor with double *Basils* about his Feet, *&c.* *Page* was carried before Sir *Francis Forbes* and committed to the same Prison for Accompanying and aiding *Sheppard* in his Escape. The prudence of Mr. *Pitt* caus'd a Separation between him and his Brother the first Night, as a Means to prevent any ensuing Danger, by having two Heads, which (according to our Proverbial Saying) *are better than one.*

The Joy the People of *Newgate* conceiv'd on this Occasion is inexpressible, *Te Deum* was Sung in the *Lodge*, and nothing but Smiles, and Bumpers, were seen there for many Days together. But *Jonathan Wild* unfortunately happen'd to be gone upon a wrong Scent after him to *Sturbridge*, and Lost a Share of the Glory.

His Escape and his being so suddenly Re-taken made such a Noise in the Town, that it was thought all the common People would have gone Mad about him; there being not a *Porter* to be had for Love nor Money, nor getting into an Ale-house, for *Butchers*; *Shoemakers* and *Barbers*, all engag'd in Controversies, and Wagers, about *Sheppard*. *Newgate* Night and Day surrounded with the Curious from St. *Giles's* and *Rag-Fair*, and *Tyburn Road* daily lin'd with Women and Children; and the *Gallows* as carefully watch'd by Night, lest he should be hang'd *Incog.* For a Report of that nature, obtain'd much upon the Rabble; In short, it was a Week of the greatest Noise and Idleness among Mechanicks that has been known in *London*, and *Parker* and *Pettis*, two *Lyricks*, subsisted many Days very comfortably upon *Ballads* and *Letters* about *Sheppard*. The vulgar continu'd under great Doubts and Difficulties, in what would be his Case, and whether the *Old Warrant*, or a *New One* must be made for his Execution, or a New Tryal, *&c.* were the great Questions as arose, and occasion'd various Reasonings and Speculation, till a News Paper, call'd the *Daily Journal* set them all to Rights by the Publication of the Account following, *viz.*

> '*J. Sheppard* having been Convicted of Burglary, and Felony, and received Sentence of Death, and afterwards 'Escap'd from *Newgate*; and being since Re-taken'; we are assur'd that it must be prov'd in a *Regular*, and *Judicial* way, that he is the same Person, who was so Convicted and made his Escape, before a Warrant can be obtain'd for his Execution; and that this Affair well be brought before the Court at the *Old Baily* the next Sessions.'

This was enough; People began to grow calm and easy and got *Shav'd*, and their Shoes *finish'd*, and Business returned into its former Channel, the Town resolving to wait the *Sessions* with Patience.

The Reverend Mr. *Wagstaff*, who officiated in the absence of the *Ordinary*, renew'd his former Acquaintance with Mr. *Sheppard*, and examin'd him in a particular manner concerning his Escape from the Condemn'd Hold: He sincerely disown'd, that all, or any, belonging to the Prison were privy thereto; but related it as it has been describ'd. He declar'd that *Edgworth Bess*, who had hitherto pass'd for his *Wife*, was not really so: This was by some thought to be in him Base, and Ungenerous in that, as she had Contributed towards his Escape, and was in Custody on that Account, it might render her more liable to Punishment, than if she had been thought his Wife; but he endeavour'd to acquit himself, by saying, that she was the sole Author of all his Misfortunes; That she betray'd him to *Jonathan Wild*, at the time he was taken in *Rosemary-Lane*; and that when he was contriving his Escape, she disobey'd his orders, as when being requir'd to attend at the Door of the Condemn'd-Hold by Nine, or Ten in the Morning to facilitate his Endeavours, she came not till the Evening, which he said, was an ungrateful Return for the care he had taken in setting her at Liberty from *New-Prison*; and thus Justify'd himself in what he had done, and said he car'd not what became of her.

He was also Examined about Mr. *Martin's* Watches; and whether *Page* was privy to that Robbery; he carefully guarded himself against uttering any thing that might affect him, peremptorily declar'd him Innocent of that, as well as of being privy to his Escape, and said, that he only out of Kindness, as being an old Companion, was resolv'd to share in his Fortunes after he had Escap'd.

He was again continually meditating a second Escape, as appear'd by his own Hardiness, and the Instruments found upon him, on *Saturday* the 12th, and *Wednesday* the 16th of *September*, the first Time a small File was found conceal'd in his Bible, and the second Time two Files, a Chisel and an Hammer being hid in the Rushes of a Chair; and whenever a Question was mov'd to him, when, or by what Means those Implements came to his Hands; he would passionately fly out, and say, *How can you? you always ask me these, and such like Questions*; and in a particular manner, when he was ask'd, Whether his Companion *Page* was an Accomplice with him, either in the affair of the Watches, or any other? (he reply'd) *That if he knew, he would give no direct Answer*, thinking it to be a Crime in him to detect the Guilty.

It was thought necessary by the Keepers to remove him from the Condemn'd-Hold to a Place, call'd the *Castle*, in the Body of the Goal, and to Chain him down to two large Iron Staples in the Floor; the Concourse of People of tolerable Fashion to see him was exceeding Great, he was always Chearful and Pleasant to a Degree, as turning almost every thing as was said into a Jest and Banter.

Being one *Sunday* at the Chapel, a Gentleman belonging to the *Lord Mayor*, ask'd a Turnkey, Which was *Sheppard*, the Man pointed to him? Says *Sheppard, yes Sir, I am the* Sheppard, *and all the Goalers in the Town are my Flock, and I cannot stir into the Country, but they are all at my Heels* Baughing, *after me, &c.*

He told Mr. *Robins*, the *City Smith*, *That he had procur'd him a small Job, and that whoever it was that put the Spikes on the Condemn'd-Hold was an honest Man, for a better peice of Metal,* says he, *I never wrought upon in my Life.*

He was loth to believe his frequent Robberies were an Injury to the Public, for he us'd to say, That *if they were ill in one Respect, they were as good in another, and that though he car'd not for Working much himself, yet he was desirous that others should not stand Idle, more especially those of his own Trade, who were always Repairing of his Breaches.*

When serious, and that but seldom, he would Reflect on his past wicked Life. He declar'd to us, that for several Years of his Apprenticeship he had an utter abhorrence to Women of the Town, and us'd to pelt them with Dirt when they have fell in his way; till a *Button-Mould-Maker* his next Neighbour left off that Business, and set up a Victualling-house in *Lewkenhors-Lane*, where himself and other young Apprentices resorted on *Sundays*, and at all other Opportunities. At this House began his Acquaintance with *Edgworth Bess*. His sentiments were strangely alter'd, and from an Aversion to those Prostitutes, he had a more favourable Opinion, and even Conversation with them, till he Contracted an ill Distemper, which as he said, he cur'd himself of by a Medicine of his own preparing.

He inveigh'd bitterly against his Brother *Thomas* for putting him into the Information, for Mrs. *Cook's* Robberry, and pretended that all the Mischiefs that attended him was owing to that Matter. He acknowledg'd that he was concern'd in that Fact, and that his said Brother broke into his Lodgings, and stole from him all his Share and more of the acquir'd Booty.

He often-times averr'd, that *William Field* was no ways concern'd in Mr. *Kneebone's* Robbery; but that being a Brother of the Quill; *Blewskin* and himself told him the particulars, and manner of the Facts, and that all he Swore against him at his Tryal was False, and that he had other Authority for it, than what came out of their (*Sheppard* and *Blewskin*) Mouths, who actually committed the Fact.

And moreover, that *Field* being acquainted with their Warehouse (a Stable) near the *Horse-Ferry* at *Westminster*, which *Sheppard* had hir'd, and usually resposited therein the Goods he stole. He came one

Night, and broke open the same, and carried off the best part of the Effects taken out of Mr. *Kneebone's* Shop.

Sheppard said he thought this to be one of the greatest Villanies that could be acted, for another to come and Plunder them of Things for which they had so honourably ventur'd their Lives, and wish'd that *Field*, as well as his Brother *Tom* might meet with forgiveness for it.

He declar'd himself frequently against the Practice of *Whidling*, or *Impeaching*, which he said, had made dreadful Havock among the *Thieves*, and much lamented the depravity of the *Brethren* in that Respect; and said that if all were but such *Tight-Cocks* as himself, the *Reputation* of the *British Thievery* might be carried to a far greater height than it had been done for many Ages, and that there would then be but little Necessity for Jaylors and Hangmen.

These and such like were his constant Discourses, when Company went up with the Turnkeys to the *Castle* to see him, and few or none went away without leaving him Money for his Support; in which he abounded, and did therewith some small Charities to the other Prisoners; however, he was abstemious and sparing enough in his Diet.

Among the many Schemes laid by his Friends, for the preserving himself after his Escape, we were told of a most Remarkable one, propos'd by an ingenious Person, who advis'd, that he might be Expeditiously, and Secretly convey'd to the Palace at *Windsor*, and there to prostrate his Person, and his Case at the Feet of a most Gracious Prince, and his Case being so very singular and new, it might in great probability move the Royal Fountain of unbounded Clemency; but he declin'd this Advice, and follow'd the Judgment and Dictates of *Butchers*, which very speedily brought him very near the Door of the *Slaughterhouse*.

On the 4th of *September*, the Day as *Joseph Ward*, and *Anthony Upton* were Executed, there was publish'd a whimsical Letter, as from *Sheppard*, to *Jack Ketch*, which afforded Diversion to the Town, and Bread to the Author, which is as followeth, *viz*.

> SIR,
>
> I Thank you for the Favour you intended me this day: I am a Gentleman, and allow

you to be the same, and I hope can forgive Injuries; fond Nature prompted, I obey'd, Oh, propitious Minute! and to show that I am in Charity, I am now drinking your Health, and a *Bon Repo* to poor *Joseph* and *Anthony.* I am gone a few Days for the Air, but design speedily to embark; and this Night I am going upon a Mansion for a Supply; it's a stout Fortification, but what Difficulties can't I encounter, when, dear *Jack*, you find that Bars and Chains are but trifling Obstacles in the way of your Friend and Servant.

JOHN SHEPPARD.

From my Residence in Terra Australi incognito.

P.S. Pray my Service to Mr. Or——— di——— y and to Mr. *App*——— ee.

On *Saturday* the 10th of *October, Anthony Lamb,* and *Thomas Sheppard*, with 95 other Felons were carried from *Newgate* on Shipboard, for Transportation to the Plantations; the last begg'd to have an opportunity given him of taking his final Leave of his Brother *John*; but this was not to be Granted, and the greatest Favour that could be obtain'd, was that on the *Sunday* before they had an Interview at the *Chapel*, but at such a distance, that they neither saluted, or shook Hands, and the Reason given for it, was that no Implements might be convey'd to *Sheppard* to assist him in making an Escape.

This, Caution seem'd to be absolutely necessary, for it appear'd soon after that *Sheppard* found Means to release himself from the Staples to which he was Chain'd in the Castle, by unlocking a great Padlock with a Nail, which he had pickt up on the Floor, and endeavour'd to pass up the Chimney, but was prevented by the stout Iron Bars fix'd in his way, and wanted nothing but the smallest File to have perfected his Liberty. When the Assistants of the Prison, came as usual with his Victuals, they began to examine his Irons; to their great Surprize they found them loose, and ready to be taken off at Pleasure. Mr. *Pitt* the Head Keeper, and his Deputies were sent for, and *Sheppard* finding this Attempt entirely frustrated, discover'd to them by what means he had got them off; and after they had search'd him, found nothing, and Lock'd and Chain'd him down again; He took up the Nail and unlocked the Padlock before their Faces; they were struck with the greatest Amazement as having never heard, or beheld the like before. He was then Handcuff'd, and more effectually Chain'd.

The next Day, the Reverend Mr. *Purney Ordinary* of the Place came from the Country to visit him, and complain'd of the sad Disposition he found him in, as Meditateing on nothing, but Means to Escape, and declining the great Duty incumbent upon him to prepare for his approaching Change. He began to Relent, and said, that since his last Effort had prov'd not Successful, he would entertain no more Thoughts of that Nature, but entirely Dispose, and Resign himself to the Mercy of Almighty God, of whom he hop'd to find forgiveness of his manifold Offences.

He said, that *Edgworth Bess* and himself kept a little Brandy-shop together in *Lewkenhors-Lane*, and once sav'd about Thirty Pounds; but having such an universal Acquaintance amongst Theives, he had frequent calls to go *Abroad*, and soon quitted that Business, and his Shop.

On *Friday* the 2d, of *October* his old Confederate *Joseph Blake* alias *Blewskin*, was apprehended and taken at a House in St. *Giles's* Parish by *Jonathan Wild*, and by Justice *Blackerby* committed to *Newgate*. *William Field* who was at his liberty, appearing and making Oath, that *Blewskin* together with *John Sheppard* and himself, committed the Burglary and Felony in Mr. *Kneebone's* House, for which *Sheppard* was Condemn'd.

The Sessions commencing at the *Old-Bailey* on *Wednesday* the 14th of *October* following, an Indictment was found against *Blewskin* for the same, and he was brought down from *Newgate* to the *Old-Bailey* to be Arraign'd in order to his Tryal; and being in the Yard within the Gate before the Court: Mr. *Wild* being there Drinking a glass of Wine with him, he said to Mr. *Wild, You may put in a word for me, as well as for another Person?* To which Mr. *Wild* reply'd, I cannot do it. *You are certainly a dead Man, and will be tuck'd up very speedily,* or words to that effect: Whereupon *Blewskin* on a sudden seiz'd Mr. *Wild* by the Neck, and with a little Clasp Knife he was provided with he cut his Throat in a very dangerous Manner; and had it not been for a

Muslin Stock twisted in several Plaits round his Neck, he had in all likelyhood succeeded in his barbarous Design before *Ballard* the Turnkey, who was at Hand, could have time to lay hold of him; the Villain trumph'd afterwards in what he had done, Swearing many bloody Oaths, that if he had murder'd him, he should have died with Satisfaction, and that his Intention was to have cut off his Head, and thrown it into the Sessions House-Yard among the Rabble, and Curs'd both his Hand and the Knife for not Executing it Effectually.

Mr. *Wild* instantly had the Assistance of three able Surgeons, *viz.* Mr. *Dobbins*, Mr. *Marten* and Mr. *Coletheart*, who sew'd up the Wound, and order'd him to his Bed, and he has continu'd ever since, but in a doubtful State of Recovery.

The Felons on the Common Side of *Newgate*, also animated by *Sheppard's* Example, the Night before they were to be Shipt for Transportation, had cut several Iron Bars assunder, and some of them had saw'd off their Fetters, the rest Huzzaing, and making Noises, under pretence of being Joyful that they were to be remov'd on the Morrow, to prevent the Workmen being heard; and in two Hours time more, if their Design had not been discover'd, near One Hundred Villians had been let loose into the World, to have committed new Depredations; nothing was wanted here but *Sheppard's* great Judgment, who was by himself in the strong Room, call'd the *Castle*, meditating his own Deliverance, which he perfected in the manner following.

On *Thursday* the 15th of this Instant *October*, at between One and Two in the Afternoon, *William Austin*, an Assistant to the Keepers, a Man reputed to be a very diligent, and faithful Servant, went to *Sheppard* in the strong Room, call'd the *Castle*, with his Necessaries, as was his Custom every Day. There went along with him Captain *Geary*, the Keeper of *New Prison*, Mr. *Gough*, belonging to the *Gatehouse* in *Westminster*, and two other Gentlemen, who had the Curiosity to see the Prisoner, *Austin* very strictly examined his Fetters, and his Hand-Cuffs, and found them very Safe; he eat his Dinner and talk'd with his usual Gayety to the Company: They took leave of him and wish'd him a good Evening. The Court being sitting at the *Old-Bailey*, the Keepers and most of their Servants were attending there with their Prisoners: And *Sheppard* was told that if he wanted any thing more, then was his Time, because they could not come to him till the next Morning: He thank'd them for their Kindness, and desir'd them to be as *early as possible*.

The same Night, soon after 12 of the Clock Mr. *Bird*, who keeps a Turners-shop adjoyning to *Newgate*, was disturb'd by the Watchman, who found his Street Door open, and call'd up the Family, and they concluding the Accident was owing to the Carelessness of some in the House, shut their Doors, and went to Bed again.

The next Morning *Friday*, at about eight Mr. *Austin* went up as usual to wait on *Sheppard*, and having unlock'd and unbolted the double Doors of the Castle, he beheld almost a Cart-load of Bricks and Rubbish about the Room, and his Prisoner gone: The Man ready to sink, came trembling down again, and was scarce able to Acquaint the People in the *Lodge* with what had happen'd.

The whole Posse of the Prison ran up, and stood like Men depriv'd of their Senses: Their surprize being over, they were in hopes that he might not have yet entirely made his Escape, and got their Keys to open all the strong Rooms adjacent to the *Castle*, in order to Trace him, when to their farther Amazement, they found the Door ready open'd to their Hands; and the strong Locks, Screws and Bolts broken in pieces, and scatter'd about the Jayl. Six great Doors (one whereof having not been open'd for seven Years past) were forc'd, and it appear'd that he had Descended from the Leads of *Newgate* by a Blanket (which he fasten'd to the Wall by an Iron Spike he had taken from the Hatch of the *Chapel*) on the House of Mr. *Bird*, and the Door on the Leads having been left open, it is very reasonable to conclude he past directly to the Street Door down the Stairs; Mr *Bird* and his Wife hearing an odd sort of a Noise on the Stairs as they lay in their Bed, a short time before the Watchman alarm'd the Family.

Infinite Numbers of Citizens came to *Newgate* to behold *Sheppard's* Workmanship, and Mr. *Pitt* and his Officers very readily Conducted them up Stairs, that the World might be convinc'd there was not the least room to suspect, either a Negligence, or Connivance in the Servants. Every one express'd the greatest Surprize that has been known, and declar'd themselves satisfy'd with the Measures they had taken for the Security of their Prisoner.

One of the Sheriffs came in Person, and went up to the *Castle* to be satisfy'd of the Situation of the Place, *&c*. Attended by several of the City Officers.

The Court being sat at the *Sessions-House*, the Keepers were sent for and Examin'd, and the Magistrates were in great Consternation, that so horrid a Wretch had escap'd their Justice. It being intended that he should have been brought down to the Court the last Day of the *Sessions*, and order'd for Execution in two or three Days after; if it appear'd that he was the Person Condemn'd for the breaking Mr. *Kneebone's* House, and included in the Warrant for Execution, *&c*.

Many of the Methods by which this miraculous Escape was effected, remain as yet a Secret, there are some indeed too Evident, the most reasonable Conjecture that has hierto been made, is, that the first Act was his twisting and breaking assunder by the strength of his Hands a small Iron Chain, which together with a great Horse Padlock, (as went from the heavy Fetters about his Legs to the staples) confin'd him to the Floor, and with a Nail open'd the Padlock and set himself at Liberty about the Room: A large flat Iron Bar appears to have been taken out of the Chimney, with the Assistance thereof 'tis plain he broke thro' a Wall of many Foot in Thickness, and made his way from the *Castle* into another strong Room Contiguous, the Door of it not having been open'd since several of the *Preston* Prisoners were Confin'd there about seven Years ago: Three Screws are visibly taken off of the Lock, and the Doors as strong as Art could make them, forc'd open. The Locks and Bolts, either wrench'd or Broke, and the Cases and other Irons made for their Security cut assunder: An Iron Spike broke off from the Hatch in the *Chapel*, which he fix'd in the Wall and fasten'd his Blanket to it, to drop on the Leads of Mr. *Bird's* House, his Stockings were found on the Leads of *Newgate*; 'tis question'd whether sixty Pounds will repair the Damage done to the Jayl.

It will perhaps be inquir'd how all this could be perform'd without his being heard by the Prisoners or the Keepers; 'tis well known that the Place of his Confinement is in the upper part of the Prison, none of the other Felons being Kept any where near him; and 'tis suppos'd that if any had heard him at Work, they would rather have facilitated, than frustrated his Endeavours. In the Course of his Breaches he pass'd by a Door on his Left belonging to the *Common-Side* Felons, who have since Curs'd him heartily for his not giving them an opportunity to kiss his Hand, and lending them a favourable lift when his Hand was in; but that was not a Work proper for Mr. *Sheppard* to do in his then Circumstances.

His Fetters are not to be found any where about the Jayl, from whence 'tis concluded he has either thrown them down some Chimney, or carried them off on his Legs, the latter seems to be Impracticable, and would still render his Escaping in such Manner the more astonishing; and the only Answer that is given to the whole, at *Newgate* is, *That the* Devil *came in Person and assisted him.*

He undoubtedly perform'd most of these Wonders in the darkest part of the Night, and without the least Glimpse of a Candle; a word, he has actually done with his own Hands in a few Hours, what several of the most skilful Artists allow, could not have been acted by a number of Persons furnish'd with proper Implements, and all other Advantages in a full Day.

Never was there anything better Tim'd, the Keepers and all their Assistants being obliged to a strict Attendance on the Sessions at the *Old Bailey*, which held for about a Week; and *Blewskin* having confin'd *Jonathan Wild* to his Chamber, a more favourable opportunity could not have presented for Mr. *Sheppard's* Purposes.

The Jaylors suffer'd much by the Opinion the ignorant Part of the People entertain'd of the Matter, and nothing would satisfie some, but that they not only Conniv'd at, but even assisted him in breaking their own Walls and Fences, and that for this Reason too, *viz.* That he should be at Liberty to instruct and train up others in his Method of House-Breaking; and replenish the Town with a new set of Rogues, to supply the Places of those Transported beyond Sea.

This is indeed a fine way of Judging, the well-known Characters of Mr. *Pitt*, and his Deputies, are sufficient to wipe of such ridiculous Imputations; and 'tis a most lamentable Truth, that they have often-times had in their Charge Villains of the deepest Die; Persons of Quality and great Worth, for whom no Entreaties, no Sums how large soever have been able to interfere between the doleful Prison, and the fatal Tree.

The Officers have done their Duty, they are but Men, and have had to deal with a Creature something more than Man, a *Protoeus*, Supernatural, Words cannot describe him, his Actions and Workmanship which are too visible, best testifie him.

On *Saturday* the 17th, *Joseph Blake*, alias *Blewskin*, came upon his Tryal at the *Old Bailey*: *Field* gave the same Evidence against him, as he had formerly done against *Sheppard*; and the Prisoner making but a triffling Defence, the Jury found him Guilty of Buglary and Felony. The Criminal when the Verdict was brought in, made his Obeysances to the Court, *and thank'd them for their Kindness.*

It will be necessary that we now return to the Behaviour of Mr. *Sheppard*, some few Days before his last Flight.

Mr. *Figg* the famous Prize Fighter comeing to see him, in *NEWGATE*, there past some pleasant Raillery between them; and after Mr. *Figg* was gone, *Sheppard* declared he had a Mind to send him a formal Challenge to Fight him at all the Weapons in the strong Room; and that let the Consequence be what it would, he should call at Mr. *Figg's* House in his way to Execution, and drink a merry Glass with him by way of Reconciliation.

A young Woman an Acquaintance of his Mother, who wash'd his Linnen and brought him Necessaries, having in an Affray, got her Eyes beaten Black and Blue; says *Sheppard* to her, *How long hast thou been Married?* Replyes the Wench. *I wonder you can ask me such a Question, when you so well know the Contrary*: Nay, says *Sheppard* again, Sarah *don't deny it, for you have gotten your Certificate in your Face.*

Mr. *Ireton* a Bailiff in *Drury-Lane* having pursued *Sheppard* after his Escape from the Condemn'd-Hold with uncommon Diligence; (for the safety of that Neighbourhood which was the chief Scene of his Villainies) *Sheppard* when Re-taken, declared, he would be even with him for it, and if ever he procur'd his Liberty again, *he would give all his Prisoners an* ACT OF GRACE. A Gentleman in a jocose way ask'd him to come and take a Dinner with him, *Sheppard* reply'd, *he accepted of the Invitation, and perhaps might take an opportunity to wait on him*; and there is great Reason to believe he has been as good as his Word.

He would complain of his Nights, as saying, *It was dark with him from Five in the Evening, till Seven in the Morning*; and being not permitted to have either a Bed or Candle, his Circumstances were dismal; and that he never slept but had some confus'd Doses, he said he consider'd all this with the Temper of a Philosopher.

Neither his sad Circumstances, nor the solemn Exhortations of the several Divines who visited him, were able to divert him from this ludicrous way of Expression; he said, *They were all Ginger-bread Fellows*, and came rather out of Curiosity, than Charity; and to form *Papers* and *Ballads* out of his Behaviour.

A *Welch* Clergyman who came pretty often, requested him in a particularly Manner to refrain Drinking; (tho' indeed there was no necessity for that Caution) *Sheppard* says, Doctor, *You set an Example and I'll follow*; this was a smart Satyr and Repartee upon the *Parson*, some Circumstances consider'd.

When he was visited in the *Castle* by the Reverend Mr. *Wagstaff*, he put on the Face only of a Preparation for his End, as appear'd by his frequent Attempts made upon his Escape, and when he has been press'd to Discover those who put him upon Means of Escaping, and furnish'd him with Implements, he would passionately, and with a Motion of striking, say, *ask me no such Questions, one File's worth all the Bibles in the World.*

When ask'd if he had not put off all Thoughts of an Escape and Entertain'd none but those of Death, would Answer by way of Question, not directly, whether they thought it possible, or probable for him to Effect his Release, when Manackled in the manner he was. When mov'd to improve the few Minutes that seem'd to remain of his Life; he did indeed listen to, but not regard the Design and Purport of his Admonition, breaking in with something New of his own, either with respect to his former Accomplices, or Actions, and all too with Pleasure and Gayety of Expression.

When in *Chapel*, he would seemingly make his Responses with Devotion; but would either Laugh, or force Expressions (when as an Auditor of the Sermon) be of Contempt, either of the Preacher, or of his Discourse.

In fine, he behav'd so, in Word, and Action, (since retaken) that demonstrated to the World, that his Escape was the utmost

Employ of his Thoughts, whatever Face of Penitence he put on when visited by the Curious.

An Account of SHEPPARD'S Adventures of five Hours immediately after his Escape from *Newgate*, in a Letter to his Friend.

DEAR FRIEND!

Over a Bottle of *Claret* you'll give me leave to *declare it*, that I've fairly put the *Vowels* upon the good Folks at *Newgate*, *i.o.u.* When I'm able, I may, or may not discharge my *Fees*, 'tis a *Fee-simple*, for a Man in my Condition to acknowledge; and tho' I'm safe out of *Newgate*, I must yet have, or at least, affect, a *New Gate* by Limping, or Turning my Toes in by making a right *Hand* of my Feet. Not *to be long*, for I hate *Prolixity* in all Business: *In short*, after *Filing, Defileing, Sawing*, when no Body *Saw*. *Climbing* (this *Clime in*) it prov'd a good *Turner* of my Affairs, thro' the House of a *Turner*. Being quite past, and safe from *Estreat* on Person or Chattels, and safe in the *Street*, I thought Thanks due to him who cou'd *Deliver hence*; and immediately (for you must know I'm a *Catholick*) to give Thanks for my Deliverance, I stept amongst the *Grey-Fryers* to come an joyn with me, in saying a *Pater-Noster*, or so, at *Amen-Corner*. The *Fryers* being *Fat* began to *Broil*, and soon after *Boild up* into a Passion to be disturb'd at that time of Night. But being got *Loose* and having no Time to *Lose*, I gave them good Words, and so the Business was done. From thence I soon slip'd through *Ludgate*, but was damnably fearful of an *Old Bailey* always lurking thereabout, who might have brought me to the *Fleet* for being too *Nimble*, besides, I was wonderfully apprehensive of receiving some unwelcome *Huggings* from the *W....n* there; therefore with a step and a stride I soon got over *Fleet-ditch*, and (as in Justice I ought) I prais'd the *Bridge* I got over. Being a *Batchelor*, and not being capable to to manage a Bridewell you know. I had no Business near *St. Brides*, so kept the right handside, designing to *Pop* into the *Alley* as usual; but fearing to go thro' there, and *harp* too much on the same *String*, it gave an *Allay* to my Intention, and on I went to *Shoe-lane* end but there meeting with a *Bully Hack* of the Town, he wou'd have shov'd me down, which my Spirit resenting, tho' a *brawny Dog*, I soon *Coller'd* him, fell Souse at him, then with his own Cane I *strapped* till he was force to *Buckle* too, and hold his *Tongue*, in so much he durst not say his *Soul* was his own, and was glad to pack of at *Last*, and turn his *Heels* upon me: I was glad he was gone you may be sure, and *dextrously* made a *Hand* of my *Feet* under the *Leg-Tavern*; but the very Thoughts of *Fetter-Lane* call'd to mind some Passages, which made me avoid the *Passage* at the end of it, (next to the Coffee House you know) so I soon whip'd over the way, yet going along two wooden *Logger-heads* at *St. Dunstan's* made just them a damn'd Noise about their *Quarters*, but the sight of me made perfectly *Hush* in a *Minute*; now fearing to goe by *Chance-a wry-Lane*, as being upon the *Watch* my self and not to be *debarr'd* at *Temple-Bar*; I stole up *Bell-Yard*, but narrowly escap'd being *Clapper-claw'd* by two Fellows I did not like in the Alley, so was forc'd to goe round with a design to *Sheer-off* into *Sheer-Lane*, but the *Trumpet* sounding at that very time, alarm'd me so, I was forc'd to Grope my way back through *Hemlock-Court*, and take my *Passage* by *Ship-Yard* without the Bar again; but there meeting with one of our trusty Friends, (all Ceremonies a-part) he told me under the *Rose* I must expect no *Mercy* in *St. Clement's* Parish, for the *Butchers* there on the *Back* on't would *Face* me, and with their *Cleavers* soon bring me down on my *marrow* Bones; you may believe I soon hastened thence, but by this time being Fainty and night Spent, I put forward, and seeing a *Light* near the *Savoy-Gate*, I was resolv'd not to make *Light* of the Opportunity, but call'd for an hearty Dram of *Luther* and *Calvin*, that is, *Mum* and *Geneva* mix'd; but having Fasted so long before, it soon got into my Noddle, and e'er I had gone twenty steps, it had so intirely *Stranded* my Reason, that by the time I came to *Half-Moon-Street* end, it gave a *New-Exchange* to my Senses, and made me quite *Lunatick.*

However, after a little Rest, I stole down *George-Passage* into *Oaf-Alley* in *York-Buildings*, and thence (tho' a vile Man) into *Villiers-Street*, and so into the *Strand* again, where having gone a little way, *Hefford's-Harp* at the Sign of the *Irish-Harp*, put me a *Jumping and Dancing* to that degree that I could not forbear making a *Somerset* or two before *Northumberland-House.* I thought once of taking the *Windsor* Coach for my self *John Sheppard*, by the Name of *Crook*—— but fearing to be *Hook'd* in before my Journey's End, I stept into *Hedge-Lane*, where two Harlots were up in the *Boughs* (it seems) *Branching* out their Respects to one another, through their Windows, and People beginning to gather thereabout, I ran *Pelmel* to *Piccadilly*, where meeting by meer chance a *Bakers* Cart going to *Turnham-Green*, I being not *Mealy Mouth'd*, nor the Man being *Crusty* I *wheel'd* out of Town.

I did call at *Hammersmith*, having no occasion directly. I shall stay two or three Days in that Neighbourhood, so, if you Direct a letter for Mr. Sligh Bolt, to be left with Mrs. *Tabitha Skymmington* at *Cheesewick*, it's Safety will *Bear Water* by any *Boat*, and come *Current* with the Tyde to

Dear BOB
Yours from the Top
of *Newgate* to the Bottom

J. *SHEPPARD*.

P.S. If you see *Blewskin*, tell him I am well, and hope he receiv'd my last—I wou'd write by the *Post* if I durst, but it wou'd be, certainly *Post-pon'd* if I did, and it would be *stranger* too, to trust a Line by a *Stranger*, who might *Palm* upon us both and never Deliver it to *Hand*.

I send this by a *Waterman*, (I dare trust) who is very Merry upon me, and says he wou'd not be in my *Jacket. Saturday Octob.* 17, 1724.

We shall conclude with what had been often observ'd by many Persons to *Sheppard*; *viz.* That it was very Imprudent in him to take Shelter in the City, or the adjacent Parts of it, after his Escape from the Condemn'd Hold; and withal to commit a *Capital Offence*, almost within Sight of *Newgate*, when his Life and all was in such Danger. His Reply was general, *viz.* That it was his Fate: But being ask'd a particular Reason for his not taking a longer Rout than the City, and the Neighbouring parts: pleaded Poverty as his Excuse for Confinement within those Limits; at the same time urging, that had he been Master at that time of five Pounds, *England* should not have been the Place of his Residence, having a good Trade in his Hands to live in any populated Part of the World.